W9-ACW-276

SIMON AND SCHUSTER BOOKS FOR YOUNG READERS

Simon & Schuster Building, Rockefeller Center, 1230 Avenue of the Americas, New York, New York 10020. Text copyright © 1989 by Maida Silverman. Illustrations copyright © 1989 by Carolyn Ewing. All rights reserved including the right of reproduction in whole or in part in any form. SIMON AND SCHUSTER BOOKS FOR YOUNG READERS is a trademark of Simon & Schuster Inc. Designed by Rebecca Tachna. Manufactured in the United States of America.

10 9 8 7 6 5 4 3 2 1

Library of Congress Cataloging-in-Publication Data

Silverman, Maida. Festival of Esther: the story of Purim. Summary: Explains the history and meaning of Purim and includes a traditional holiday song and a recipe for hamantaschen cookies. 1. Purim—Juvenile literature. 2. Purim. I. Ewing, C. S., ill. II. Title. BM695.P8S53 1989; ISBN 0-671-67200-2; ISBN 0-671-67663-6 (Pbk). 88-18601

"A Wicked, Wicked Man" is reprinted from *The Complete Family Guide to Jewish Holidays* by Dalia Hardof Renberg. Used by permission of Adama Books, New York. The author wishes to thank Ms. Judith Muffs of the Anti-Defamation League of B'nai Brith for her assistance.

FESTIVAL OF
E·S·T·H·E·R

DISCARD

◆ THE STORY OF PURIM ◆

RETOLD BY MAIDA SILVERMAN
ILLUSTRATED BY CAROLYN S. EWING

A Little Simon Book
Published by Simon & Schuster Inc., New York

J
296.4
S

Long ago, a king named Ahasuerus ruled a land called Persia. Many Jews had come there, and they lived with the Persians in peace and harmony.

One day King Ahasuerus gave a banquet for all the people in Shushan, his capital city. When the merriment was at its height, the king wanted to show off the beauty of his queen, Vashti. He ordered her to appear before his guests.

Vashti did not like to be ordered around as if she were a servant. She refused to obey the king's command.

King Ahasuerus was furious. "Not even the queen may defy me!" he cried. And he ordered Vashti banished from his kingdom.

King Ahasuerus decided to find a new queen. He sent for his
officers. "Find the fairest young women in my kingdom," he
said. "Bring them to the palace. I will choose the one who
pleases me most and make her queen."

Among those chosen by the officers was a Jewish girl
named Esther. She was an orphan who lived with her cousin
Mordecai. He had adopted Esther and raised her as if she were
his daughter.

Esther did not care about becoming a queen. She did not want to leave her cousin and her home.

"You must obey the king's order," Mordecai told her. And so Esther was taken away to the King's palace.

Many young women were brought before King Ahasuerus. None pleased him. But when he saw Esther, he fell in love with her beauty and gentleness, and chose her to be Queen of Persia.

Mordecai was the king's scribe. He wrote letters for the king. He sat in the palace courtyard, and he and Esther sent messages to each other. One day Mordecai heard two guards whispering nearby. He overheard them plotting to murder the king and take over the throne. Mordecai quickly sent a message to Esther. She told King Ahasuerus about the plot, and the guards were punished. Mordecai had saved the king's life.

Among the noblemen at court was a man named Haman, King Ahasuerus's chief advisor. Except for the king, he was the most powerful man in Persia. Everyone had to bow down to him when he passed. One morning Haman came to the palace. Everyone bowed low except for one man, who stood straight and tall.

Haman was very angry. "Who are you?" he demanded. "How dare you stand, when all must bow down to me?"

"My name is Mordecai," the man answered. "I am a Jew. Jews shall never bow down to men, as if to worship them!"

Mordecai's words filled Haman with hatred and rage. *I will revenge myself upon the Jews,* he promised himself.

Haman hurried to see the king. "There are people in Persia who ignore your laws," he said. "They are a great danger to your kingdom. Let me deal with them."

King Ahasuerus often left important matters to Haman, and believed what he said. "Do with them as you think best," he replied.

Haman sent a royal decree throughout the kingdom:
"The Jews of Persia shall be put to death. I have cast lots, and chosen the thirteenth day of the month of Adar. On that day, all will die!"

When the Jews heard the decree, they cried out in horror. They tore their clothes and rubbed their bodies with ashes as signs of grief. Mordecai rushed to the palace to see the queen. Esther wept when she heard the terrible news.

"You are Queen of Persia," Mordecai said. "Go to the king and beg him to spare us!"

"I dare not go unless I am summoned," Esther told him. "Whoever does so now is put to death."

"You must go," Mordecai pleaded. "Only you can save the Jews!"

"You are right," Esther answered. "I would rather disobey the king and die than let my people perish!"

Queen Esther took no food or drink for three days. At the end of that time, she had thought of a plan. Gathering her courage, she went to see the king.

King Ahasuerus was enraged when he saw Esther. "You dare to approach me without being summoned!" he shouted. "You know to do so means death!"

Esther was so frightened that she fainted at the king's feet.

King Ahasuerus took Esther in his arms and held her until she opened her eyes. "I'll never harm you," he said, for he truly loved Esther. "Why did you risk your very life to see me? Whatever your request, I promise to grant it."

The king's words gave Esther hope. "Tonight and tomorrow night I shall make a banquet for you and for Haman also. And tomorrow night, my king, you shall hear my request."

Haman was pleased to be honored by Queen Esther. On his way home after the first banquet, he again passed Mordecai at the palace gate. As before, Mordecai stood straight and tall. Haman's fury grew even greater. *I'll have a gallows built immediately!* he told himself. *Tomorrow Mordecai shall be hanged from it.*

Later that night, King Ahasuerus was reading his *Book of Good Deeds*. He came to the story of how Mordecai had saved his life. "How was Mordecai rewarded?" the king asked his servant.

"You did not reward him," the servant replied.

Just then Haman arrived. He planned to ask the king to hang Mordecai. But before he could speak, the king said, "There is a man I wish to honor. What do you suggest?"

King Ahasuerus must want to honor me, Haman thought, so he said, "Dress the man in fine robes and jewels, and set him on a splendid horse to be led through the streets of Shushan."

"Excellent!" said the king. "You yourself shall do all this for Mordecai."

Haman was furious, but he hid his anger and did as the king commanded.

That evening, Haman and King Ahasuerus attended the second banquet. When it was over, Queen Esther spoke. "A royal decree has been proclaimed. All the Jews of Persia

are to be killed. I, too, am a Jew," she said. "And Mordecai
is my cousin. If my people must die, I must die with them.
Oh, king, spare the lives of the Jews! This is my request."

"Who has ordered this," the king demanded.

"Haman!" Esther cried.

King Ahasuerus looked at his chief advisor, who was cowering near a window that overlooked the palace gardens. Through the window, the king saw a gallows, towering above the trees. "Who built that?" he demanded.

"Haman built it to hang Mordecai," a servant answered.

"Then Haman himself shall hang from it!" the king commanded.

And it was done.

"Even though I am a king, I cannot change a royal decree," King Ahasuerus told Esther. "But I shall grant your request in a different way. Let the Jews take up arms and defend themselves."

And so on the thirteenth day of Adar, the Jews rose up and defeated the soldiers Haman had sent to destroy them. King Ahasuerus made Mordecai his chief advisor in Haman's place.

Mordecai sent a special message to all the Jews of Persia:
"Today we were saved from Haman, who tried to destroy us and
was destroyed himself. Tomorrow is the fourteenth day of
Adar. We shall call that day Purim, and celebrate it always, with
festivity and joy!"

The Story of a Holiday

The story told in the Book of Esther took place in Persia (now Iran) around 500 B.C.E. The Purim story is described in the *Megillat Esther,* or Scroll of Esther. *Megillah* means "scroll." Long ago, books were written on rolls of paper, called scrolls.

The word *Purim* comes from an ancient word, *pur,* meaning "lots." In ancient times, if a person wanted to decide something important, he or she often tossed small objects—such as stones —onto the ground. This was called "casting lots." The pattern the lots made on the ground helped the person who cast them make decisions.

Haman cast lots made from small stones in order to decide what day and month to pick for the destruction of the Jews of Persia. This is why Purim is also called "The Feast of Lots."

Purim begins at sundown on the thirteenth day of the Hebrew month of Adar, usually in March. Many Jews do not eat or drink on this day in honor of Queen Esther, who did not eat or drink for three days before she asked King Ahasuerus to spare her people. The fifteenth day of Adar is called Shushan Purim because some Jews were still fighting Haman's soldiers on that day.

At sundown on the thirteenth day of Adar, and again the next morning, Jewish families go to the synagogue to hear the *Megillah* read aloud. On Purim, making noise is encouraged, even in the synagogue. Everyone waits for Haman's name to be mentioned. As soon as it is, children twirl groggers (rattles that make a loud, grinding noise), hit sticks together, and shout. Adults stamp their feet. This is done to fulfill the command: "May his name be blotted out!"

Purim is a holiday filled with happiness. On the fourteenth day of Adar, Jewish schools, centers, and synagogues have Purim celebrations. There are parties, masquerades, parades, and plays that tell the story of Esther. Children and even adults dress in all kinds of costumes, paint their faces, and put on masks.

At home, the family gathers for a festive afternoon meal called *Purim seudah,* or Purim feast. And Purim would not be Purim without special cookies called *hamantaschen* for dessert.

Children like to help prepare and distribute Purim gifts called *shalach manot*—plates of cookies, cakes, and candy—to neighbors, relatives, and friends. It's important to bring *shalach manot* to the poor, the elderly, and people who are alone so they, too, may enjoy Purim.

Whenever a Jewish community escaped disaster, the rabbis allowed the community to make that day a special Purim, and celebrate it every year. There are many such Purims in Jewish history. There are even "family Purims." When a particular family has been saved from a terrible fate, that family makes it a custom to celebrate its own very special Purim. The Purim celebrating the events in the Book of Esther are echoed in special Purims celebrated today.

Hamantaschen

Purim would not be complete without hamantaschen. No one is sure how these cookies got their name. Some say their triangular shape resembles the three-cornered hat worn by Haman when he was chief advisor to King Ahasuerus. In Hebrew they are called *oznei haman,* or "Haman's ears."

Dough

1 cup sugar
$1/3$ cup vegetable oil
3 large eggs
grated rind of 1 lemon
$1/2$ teaspoon vanilla
3 cups flour
2 teaspoons baking powder

Filling

1 pound cooked prunes,
  pitted and chopped
$1/2$ cup chopped walnuts
1 tablespoon lemon juice
1 tablespoon sugar

Mix first 5 ingredients together in large bowl until well blended. Add flour and baking powder. Stir to form dough. Cover dough; chill in refrigerator for 3 hours. To make filling, mix all ingredients together, blending well. Preheat oven to 375°. Form dough into a ball. Cut ball in half, roll out each half $1/8$-inch thick on lightly floured board. Cut into 3-inch circles with cookie cutter. Spoon 1 teaspoon filling in center of each circle (figure 1). Fold dough and pinch edges as shown (figure 2). Form triangle-shaped hamantaschen (figure 3). Place cookies 1 inch apart on lightly oiled cookie sheets. Bake 12–15 minutes, or until golden. Yield: approximately 3½ dozen.

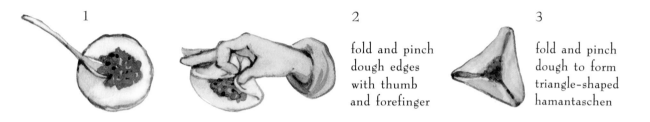

1

2

fold and pinch dough edges with thumb and forefinger

3

fold and pinch dough to form triangle-shaped hamantaschen

A Wicked, Wicked Man

Oh, once there was a wick-ed, wick-ed man And Ha - man was his

name, sir. He would have mur - dered all the Jews Though

they were not to blame, sir. Oh, to - day we'll mer-ry, mer - ry be.

Oh, to - day we'll mer - ry, mer - ry be. Oh, to - day we'll

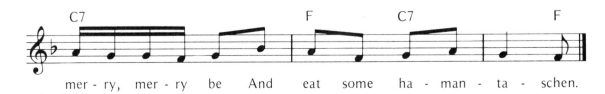

mer - ry, mer - ry be And eat some ha - man - ta - schen.